START-A-CRAFT

Puppets

Get started in a new craft with easy-to-follow

projects for beginners

DEBORAH SCHNEEBELI-MORRELL

CHARTWELL
BOOKS, INC.

A QUINTET BOOK

Published by Chartwell Books
A Division of Book Sales, Inc.
114 Northfield Avenue
Edison, New Jersey 08837

ISBN 0-7858-1007-2

This book was designed and produced by
Quintet Publishing Limited
6 Blundell Street
London N7 9BH

Creative Director: Richard Dewing
Designer: James Lawrence
Project Editor: Stefanie Foster
Photographer: Heini Schneebeli

DEDICATION
For my father David
D.S.M.

Typeset in Great Britain by
Central Southern Typesetters, Eastbourne
Manufactured in Hong Kong by
Regent Publishing Services Limited
Printed in China

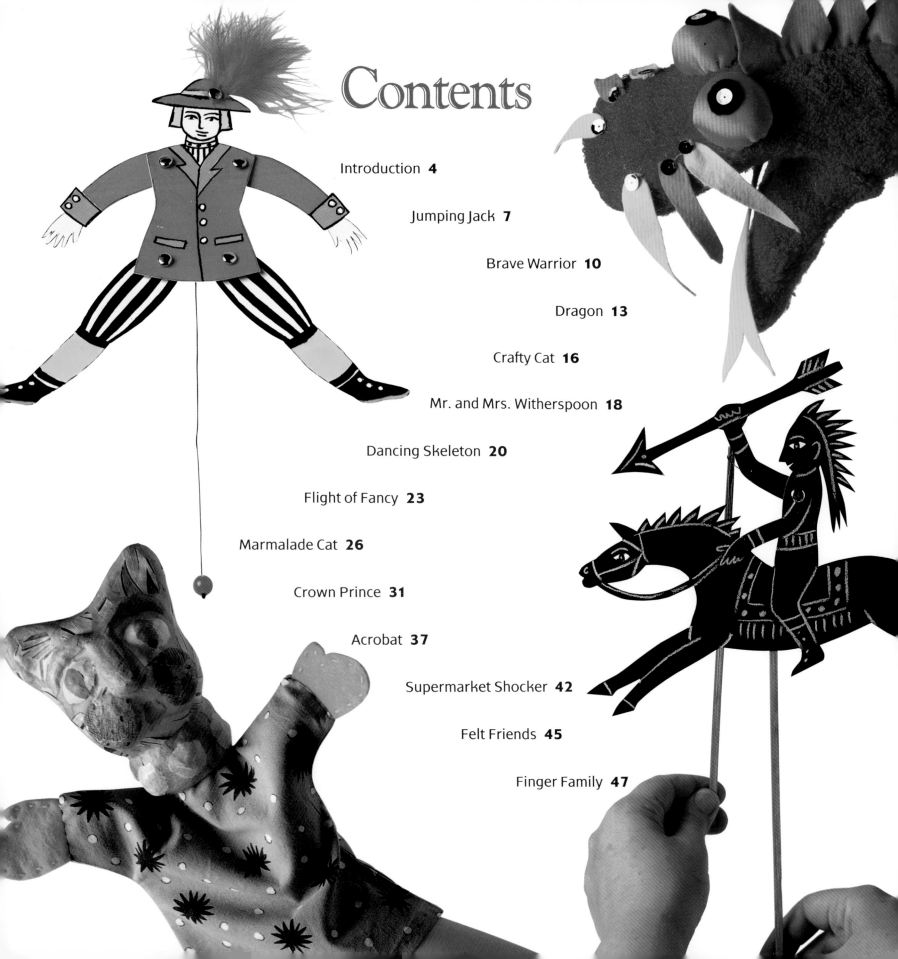

Contents

Introduction

· · ·

Puppetry holds a fascination for adults and children alike, with a universal appeal rooted in the ancient history and traditions of many cultures.

History and traditions

The oldest form of theater in the world, puppetry is widely believed to have its origins in the Far East. In both India and China puppets were used to recount legends and folk tales, and to dramatize religious and moral teachings, and it was a popular art both in the street and the Palace.

Most famous, perhaps, of the eastern puppets are the Waylang Purwa shadow puppets of Indonesia, made from beautifully painted and gilded oiled parchment. These were animated in front of a light to cast shadows on a translucent screen, depicting stories of gods, demons, and heroes. The Egyptian, Greek, and Roman cultures, too, all used some form of puppetry to represent their gods and legends.

Because puppeteers were itinerant nomadic people, their stories and traditions traveled from land to land. In the Middle Ages, the art became more prevalent in Europe, and one of the most famous examples is the commedia dell' arte in Italy in the 15th century. Possibly the most widely known puppet show in the British Isles, Punch and Judy, originated in Italy as Pulcinella. A moral tale, its stories are still faithfully acted out today, often with references to current life.

For many years during the seventeenth-century rule of Oliver Cromwell, the influence of Puritanism closed many British theaters. Puppetry kept the art alive — as it was performed by street entertainers and fairground folk, it was difficult to supress and often contained some satirical references to contemporary society.

Puppetry today

Puppets have always had the capability of expressing subtle human emotions. Although they are usually made from simple, everyday materials, they seem to come alive when operated and draw the audience into a rich world of imagination. They can often reduce the most sophisticated of people to tears of laughter! Puppetry is still very much alive in our culture in its traditional form, passed on from generation to generation, and, in a contemporary form, it is very often used in television and in animated film.

Most people will at some stage in their life have had an opportunity to make a puppet, most probably a clumsy attempt at school. Puppets made by children often have a charming and endearing naive quality that adults find impossible to reveal in their own work — they often seem to be more concerned with the technique and forget that they are trying to portray a character.

Before beginning to make puppets yourself, it is always worth looking at historic examples of the craft. Many examples exist in museums and theatrical collections, and viewing can be most inspiring and helpful. You will be adding your ideas and inventions to a long historical tradition.

The Projects

· · ·

This book consists of 13 exciting puppet projects which are inspired by traditional culture and the world of folk traditions, but which interpret the techniques, making them simple and accessible for all.

Puppet Types

There are basically four main types of puppet. Most of the projects in this book fit into these traditional categories, but there should be no doctrinaire rules about how to make them.

1. Stick Puppets

These are the simplest kinds of puppet. They generally don't actually move themselves, but are held by a stick or handle which can be moved to make simple upward and downward or sideways gestures. Examples of stick puppets in this book are the wonderfully simple wooden spoon puppets, the birds on sticks, the cardboard cat mask. The inventive variation, the Dancing Skeleton, is operated with a stick from behind while the arms, legs, and head bounce around independently as they are attached to the body with springs.

2. Glove Puppets

These are usually soft-bodied puppets which are operated by inserting a hand into its body, with the little finger and the thumb operating the arms. This kind of puppet can be very simple; the five-fingered glove puppet and the felt finger puppets are the easiest examples to make. A more traditional puppet of this kind is the Crown Prince – its head is made of papier-mâché, and a sewn body and legs are stuffed and attached to the front of the tunic. The Marmalade Cat is an example of the most common form of glove puppet. The sock Dragon is very effective in that the whole hand and forearm fits into the sock and brings the dragon to life when it is manipulated.

A more unusual and topical variety of the traditional glove puppet is the Supermarket Shocker – a plastic bottle and discarded household materials make a haunting alien masklike puppet which is operated by putting a hand into the bottle from behind.

= 5 =

4. Shadow Puppets

These are usually flat silhouettes of cardboard, the arms or legs jointed and moved with thin rods. The figure is held upright with another thin stick and operated against a translucent screen. A light is shone behind the puppet, and there should be some degree of darkness in front of the screen for dramatic effect. The Brave Warrior on a horse is a good example of a shadow puppet, but can of course be operated without light and screen to good effect.

The Jumping Jack doesn't strictly fit into any of these four categories. Perhaps more of a mechanical toy, it has most in common with the shadow puppets, and it could be used as such if a holding stick was attached to it.

A NOTE ON PAPIER-MÂCHÉ PULP

● All the materials that are listed for each project are inexpensive and readily available. Commercial pulp is available from craft or good toy stores. You may like to try making your own using the following method.

● Tear a newspaper into small squares, approximately $3/4 \times 3/4$ inches and put it all in a large saucepan. Cover with water and boil until the paper begins to disintegrate. Turn off the heat and allow to cool. Then mash with a potato masher, strain the excess water, and squeeze the rest out with your hands.

● Add $1/2$ cup of white glue, a sprinkling of dry cellulose or starch paste, $1/2$ cup of commercial wall filler, and 1 cup of fine sawdust. Knead this mixture as you would bread, on a flat surface, until all the ingredients are well mixed. This mixture will keep for a number of weeks in the refrigerator.

● The projects on the following pages provide simple, clear instructions for making the puppets. They are really easy to follow and require no special equipment or knowledge — all can be made on the kitchen table.

● As you make these projects, new and original ideas will occur to you — try them out, invent your own characters, and keep alive one of the most enduring forms of international theater!

3. String Puppets

There is strictly only one puppet in the book which fits into this category — The Acrobat. The figure is jointed at neck, elbows, waist, and knees. The limbs and head are attached with strings to a wooden cross held horizontally above the puppet. By tilting the cross, you can make the puppet move most realistically — walking, jumping, dancing, or turning the head. This is the most sophisticated technique in puppet making, but the Acrobat in this book is much simplified and needs only careful attention and patience to produce a very effective example of this method.

Jumping Jack

This traditional puppet is seen in many cultures, and something like it was perhaps the first moving toy to be made. We have made a simple version – with a feather in its cap – but the same principle can be used to make very complicated puppets with many moving parts.

You will need
◊ Tracing paper
◊ Pencil
◊ Thin ivory-colored cardboard
◊ Scissors
◊ Felt-tipped pens (yellow, black, orange, and pink)
◊ Hole punch
◊ 5 paper brads
◊ Strong black thread
◊ Feather
◊ Clear all-purpose glue
◊ Small wooden or glass bead

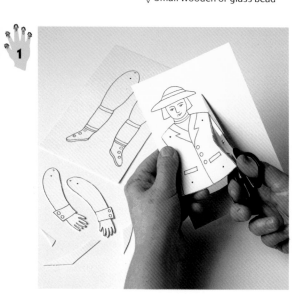

1 Transfer the template images to the cardboard and carefully cut out the arms, legs, and body.

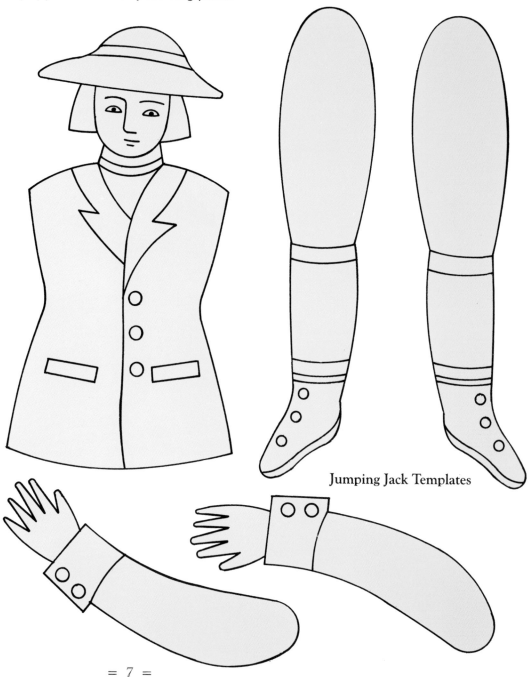

Jumping Jack Templates

2 Color the hair, hat band, lower legs, and soles of the shoes yellow.

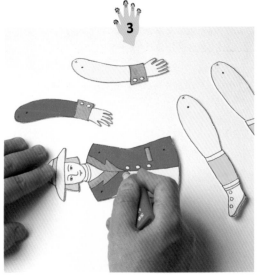

3 Color the jacket and hat in pink and orange, using the illustration of the finished puppet for reference.

4 Color the black areas of the boots and the striped breeches.

5 Pierce the holes shown on the template — one each at the shoulders and hips and two at the top of both arms and both legs.

6 Attach the arms and the legs to the body with paper brads, making sure that the limbs move freely before you turn back the tabs on the fasteners.

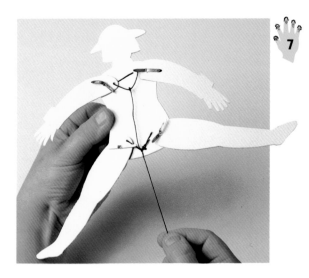

7 Thread the black thread through the other holes in the arms and the legs.

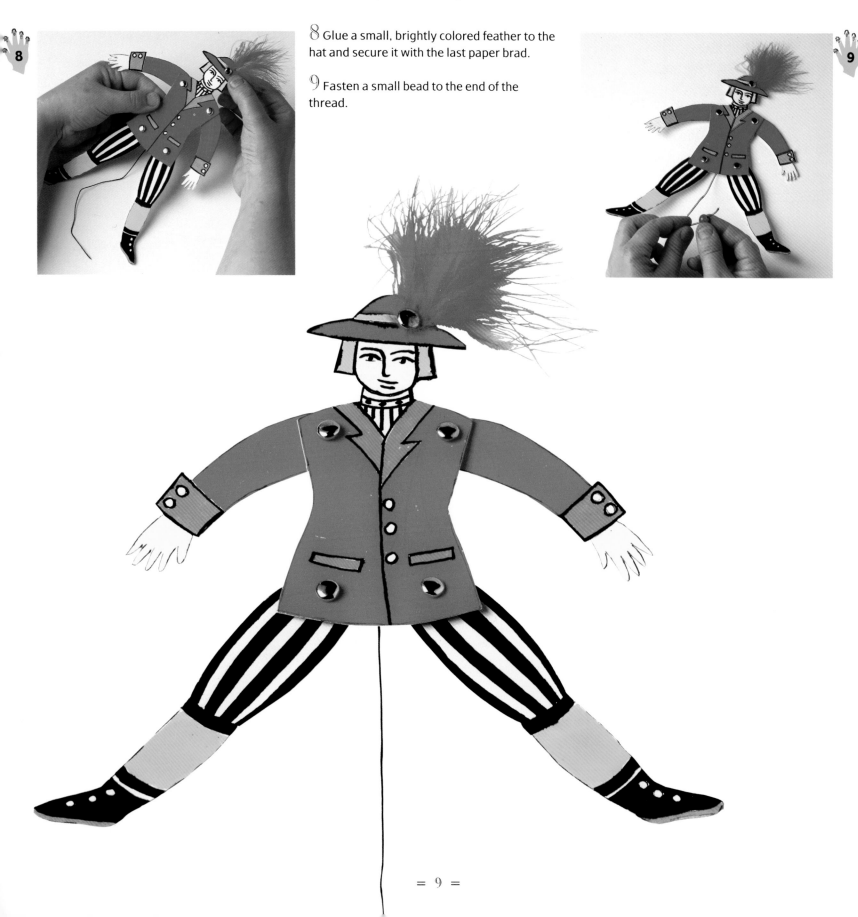

8 Glue a small, brightly colored feather to the hat and secure it with the last paper brad.

9 Fasten a small bead to the end of the thread.

Brave Warrior

· · ·

This plucky Native American, inspired by folk-art weather vanes, is easy to make and even easier to operate. You can use the same method to create more characters so that you can act out a complete drama.

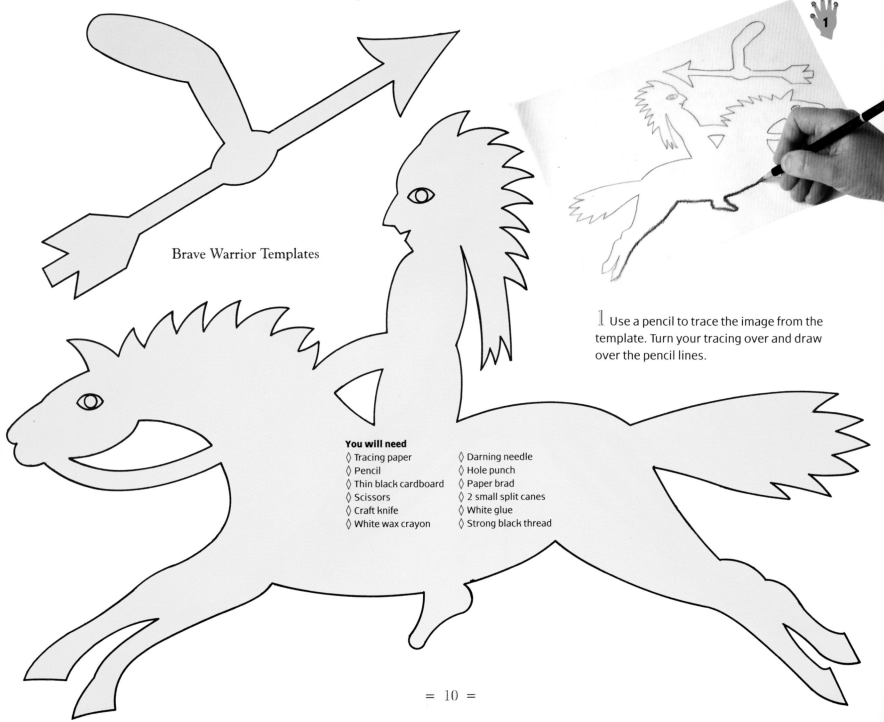

Brave Warrior Templates

1 Use a pencil to trace the image from the template. Turn your tracing over and draw over the pencil lines.

You will need
◊ Tracing paper
◊ Pencil
◊ Thin black cardboard
◊ Scissors
◊ Craft knife
◊ White wax crayon
◊ Darning needle
◊ Hole punch
◊ Paper brad
◊ 2 small split canes
◊ White glue
◊ Strong black thread

2 Turn over the tracing paper again and carefully draw over the original traced lines with a sharp pencil to transfer the image to the black cardboard. Remove the tracing paper.

3 Accurately cut out the image.

4 Use a craft knife to cut out the parts that are not accessible with scissors – under the arms, for example.

5 Cut out the eyes with the point of your craft knife.

6 Highlight the image with a sharp white crayon. Don't forget to add the detail to the arm and arrow.

7 Use a darning needle to pierce a hole through the elbow of the arm carrying the arrow.

8 Position the arrow-carrying arm behind the body and pierce a hole through both thicknesses at the "shoulder."

9 Push a paper brad through the holes, making sure that the arm can be moved before you open out the tabs on the back.

10 Glue one piece of split cane to the center of the back of the horse.

11 Make a small hole in the top of the other piece of cane and tie it loosely to the elbow with strong black thread.

Dragon

Don't throw away your old or odd socks. You can turn them into a host of colorful characters — monsters, a dragon like this one, or anything that captures your imagination — and watch them metamorphose into a new existence.

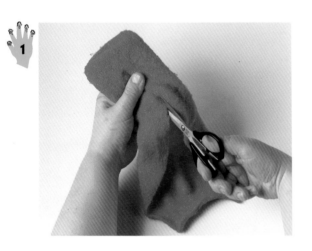

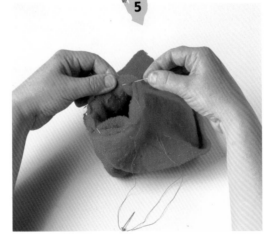

You will need
◊ Sewing thread
◊ 2 old socks
◊ Pins
◊ Scissors
◊ Needle
◊ Felt (orange, black, yellow, and pink)
◊ Polyester stuffing
◊ Scrap material (for eyes)
◊ Fabric glue
◊ Sequins

1 Cut a slit down the back of one sock and a little way along the sole.

2 Cut a slit in the same sock on the upper foot and opposite the heel.

3 Cut off the toe of the other sock.

4 With right sides together, pin the toe section into the slit in the first sock.

5 Stitch the toe section in place to make the lower jaw.

6 Cut out a zigzag from the orange felt. It should be approximately 12 inches long.

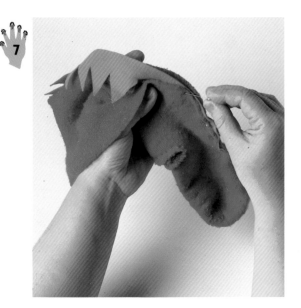

7 Still with the sock inside out, place the zigzag along the slit up the back, pinning it so that the straight edge of the zigzag lies along the slit and the points lie inward.

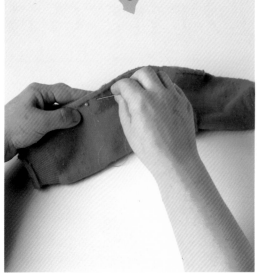

8 Use running stitch to sew the zigzag in place.

9 Pull the sock right side out, to reveal the fins running down the back.

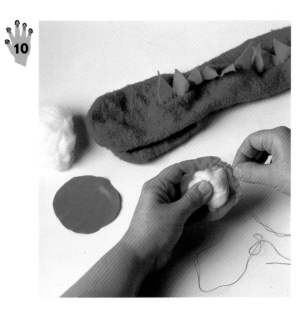

10 Stitch a neat line of small running stitches around the edge of a circle of pink fabric; do not fasten off the thread. Place a small wad of polyester stuffing in the center.

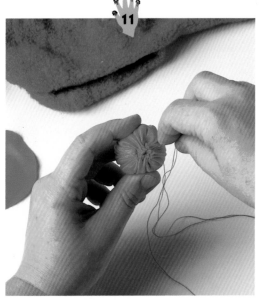

11 Pull up the running stitches to form a ball and overcast to hold.

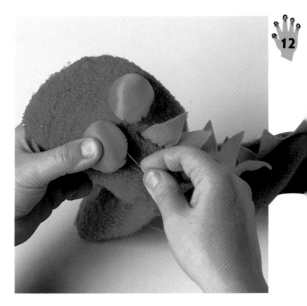

12 Sew the eyeballs onto the sock head, just in front of the end of the fins.

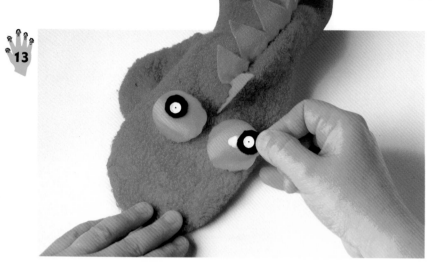

13 Use fabric glue to stick white sequins onto small circles of black felt. Stick the "eyes" onto the eyeballs.

14 Sew on scraps of orange, yellow, and pink felt as whiskers, and glue sequins onto the ends at the points where they are sewn to the head.

15 Cut out a forked tongue from yellow felt and sew it inside the mouth. Slide your arm into the sock, putting your thumb into the lower jaw.

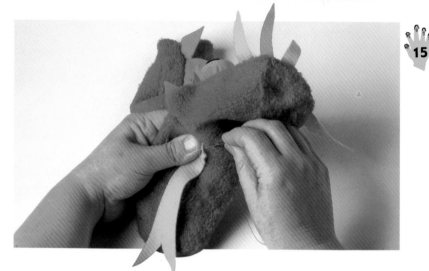

Crafty Cat

This is one of the easiest stick puppets you can make – it's simply a cardboard shape on a stick. We have used the idea of a mask, a shape cut from cardboard and then painted to create a striking image.

You will need
◊ Thin cardboard (from a cereal box, for example)
◊ Felt-tipped pen (black)
◊ Scissors
◊ Craft knife
◊ Acrylic primer (white)
◊ Paintbrush
◊ Acrylic paint (green, white, blue, orange, and yellow)
◊ All-purpose glue
◊ Flat stick

1 Draw a cat's head on cardboard with a black felt-tipped pen and cut around the outline with scissors.

2 Use a craft knife to cut out the slits for the eyes and mouth.

3 Paint a coat of acrylic primer over the whole face.

4 When the primer is dry, paint the face bright green.

5 Paint the nose blue, adding white highlights.

6 Outline the eyes and mouth in blue, then paint a white circle on each side of the nose for cheeks.

= 16 =

7 Paint some yellow shading on the cheeks to give a three-dimensional effect and then add some orange dots.

8 Paint white inner ears, add yellow and orange stripes under the eyes, and add a chin. Finally, edge the entire mask with blue.

9 Glue the stick firmly in place on the back of the mask.

Mr. and Mrs. Witherspoon

• • •

Wooden spoons are inexpensive and available in a variety of shapes and sizes. They always seem to impart a slightly prim feeling to the puppet faces. Use the method described here to make a whole cast of characters, or an entire family.

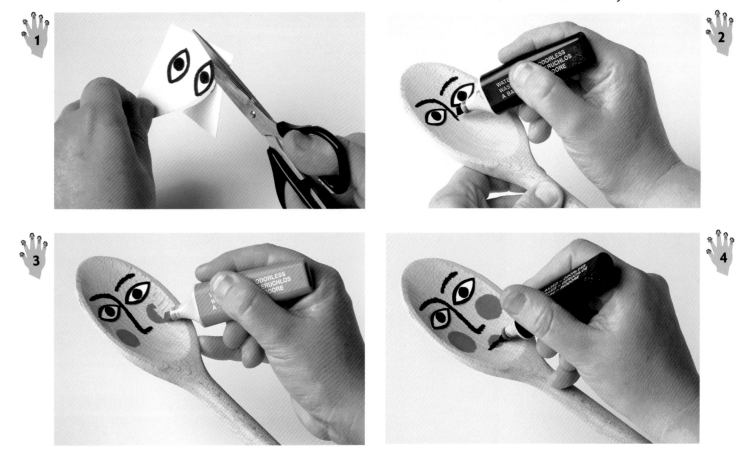

You will need
◊ White typing paper or thin cardboard
◊ Felt-tipped pens (black, pink, and blue)
◊ Scissors
◊ 1 wooden spoon
◊ Clear, all-purpose glue
◊ Stage hair (we used red)
◊ Sequins
◊ Ribbon

1 Use a black felt-tipped pen to draw two eyes on the white paper. Carefully cut out the eyes with scissors.

2 Glue the eyes to the wooden spoon, about one-third of the way from the top. Draw in the eyebrows and nose with black felt-tipped pen.

3 Use a pink felt-tipped pen to add the cheeks.

4 Draw in the mouth with pink felt-tipped pen and add a black line. Finish the face with some blue eyeshadow.

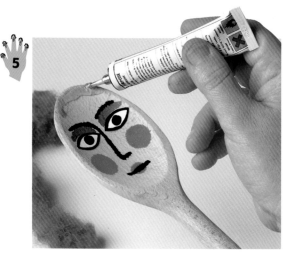

5 Smear some adhesive along the top edge of the spoon.

6 Glue on the stage hair.

7 Glue a large green sequin on each side of the face, partly on the spoon and partly on the hair.

8 Tie the ribbon in a neat bow around the neck of the puppet and trim to length.

Dancing Skeleton

• • •

This little puppet was inspired by the Day of the Dead Festival, when Mexicans eat candy shaped like skulls. It's a simple puppet to make, but it dances in a macabre yet entertaining way. Use a ready-made papier-mâché pulp if you do not want to make your own.

You will need
◊ Papier-mâché pulp
◊ Knife
◊ 1 piece of ¼-inch dowel, 12 inches long
◊ 2 springs, each 5 inches long
◊ 2 springs, each 3½ inches long
◊ 1 spring, 1½ inches long
◊ Acrylic primer (white)
◊ Paintbrushes (medium and small)
◊ Acrylic paint (gray)

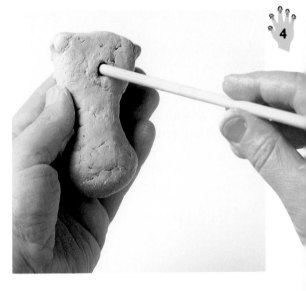

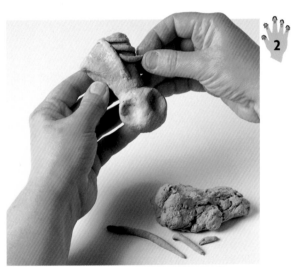

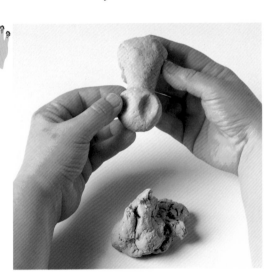

1 Model the body of the skeleton from papier-mâché pulp with your hands, narrowing the waist and pinching out the pelvis.

2 Roll out small sausage shapes from pulp and arrange them to form the ribs on the upper body.

3 Use a paring knife to model the vertebrae.

4 Push the pieces of dowel into the back of the skeleton's body to a depth of about ½ inch.

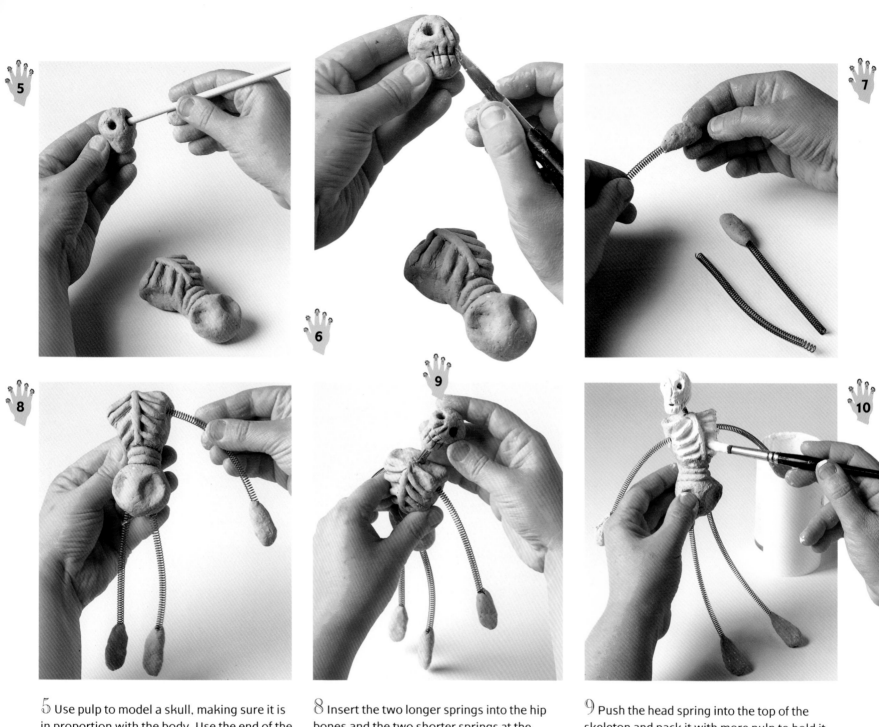

5 Use pulp to model a skull, making sure it is in proportion with the body. Use the end of the dowel to create eye sockets.

6 Use a knife to draw in the jaw and to make indentations to represent the teeth.

7 Press small amounts of pulp onto the ends of the four long springs to form the hands and feet. Insert the small spring into the base of the skull.

8 Insert the two longer springs into the hip bones and the two shorter springs at the shoulders of the skeleton body. The springs should go into the body to a depth of about ½ inch. Pack the springs with pulp, so that they are firmly embedded in the pulp.

9 Push the head spring into the top of the skeleton and pack it with more pulp to hold it firm. As the pulp dries, it will help to hold the springs in place. Leave the skeleton to dry in a warm place – an oven on a very low setting is suitable.

10 When the skeleton is completely dry, give the body, skull, hands, and feet a coat of white primer. Take care that you do not get paint on the springs.

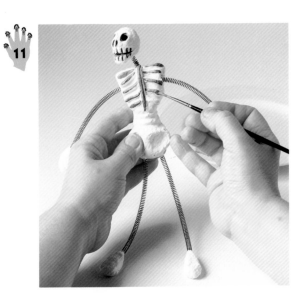

11 Leave the primer to dry, then paint the outlines of the rib bones, eye sockets, jaw, teeth, and pelvis in gray paint.

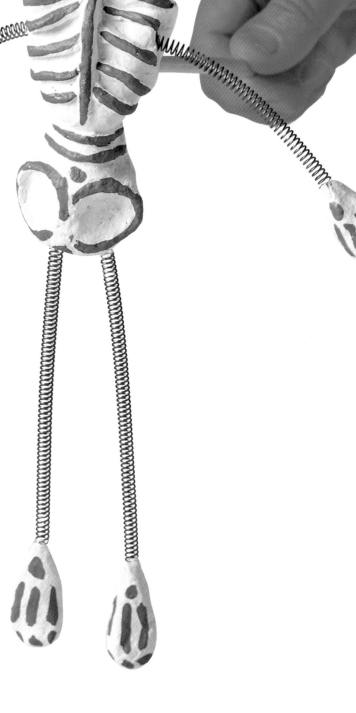

12 Paint in the outlines of the bones in the hands and feet in the same way.

13 Push the dowel into the hole in the back. If you wish you can use a spot of glue to hold it, but you may prefer to leave it so that you can take it out.

Flight of Fancy

· · ·

Have you ever wondered what you can do with all the corks that you find left over after a party? Well, here's one answer — make a flock of birds. This is possibly the easiest of all the projects in the book, and one that might lead to your own flights of fancy. Try adding real feathers or sequins or use glittery paper.

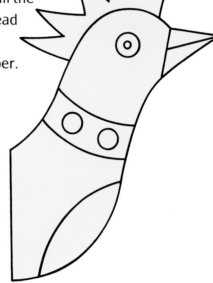

Flight of Fancy Templates

Templates for the tail and head of the birds.

You will need
◊ Tracing paper
◊ Pencil
◊ Thin white cardboard
◊ Felt-tipped pens (yellow, orange, pink, blue, red, and black)
◊ Scissors
◊ Craft knife
◊ Cork
◊ 1 piece of ¼-inch dowel, approximately 14 inches long

1 Transfer the outlines of the template to the white cardboard, then, using the illustration of the finished puppet as a guide, begin to color in the bird's head and tail with yellow and orange.

2 Use red for the crest and comb and blue to color the face. Outline the beak and eyes in black.

3 Carefully add the pink spots to the tail.

4 When you have finished coloring, neatly cut out the head and tail.

5 Use a craft knife to cut a slit, about ¼ inch deep, across each end of the cork.

6 Use the point of a pair of closed scissors to make a hole in the bottom of the cork.

7 Insert the dowel into the hole in the cork.

8 Holding the dowel, color the side of the cork blue and the ends pink.

9 Push the head and tail sections into the slits you have cut in the ends of the cork.

Marmalade Cat

· · ·

This puppet is made using the simple papier-mâché layering technique. Instead of decorating with paint, the cat's face is created using torn scrap paper. In this way the construction and decoration of the puppet are part of the same process.

Tunic Template

Use this template to cut out two pieces of material for the tunic.

You will need
◊ Modeling clay (blue and yellow)
◊ Petroleum jelly
◊ Construction paper (blue and orange; small amounts of yellow and green)
◊ Colorful wrapping paper (scraps)
◊ Paste (cellulose or starch)
◊ Craft knife
◊ White glue
◊ Masking tape
◊ Cardboard tube
◊ Tracing paper

◊ Pencil
◊ Scissors
◊ Pins
◊ Scrap material, approximately 12 inches square × 2
◊ Pins
◊ Needle
◊ Sewing thread
◊ Orange felt, approximately 12 inches square × 2
◊ Orange embroidery floss

Cut out four mitten pieces using this template.

Mitten Template

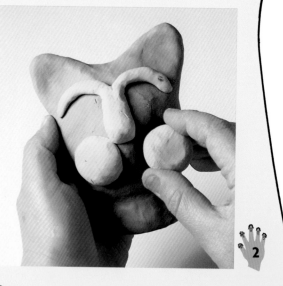

1 Model the blue clay into a cat's head shape.

2 Using the yellow modeling clay, make the features — the nose, eyebrows, and two balls for the cheeks.

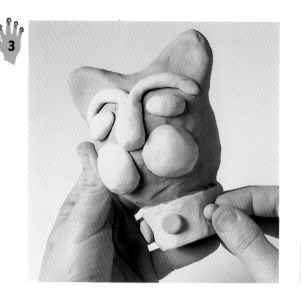

3 Make a collar from yellow modeling clay and add blue bobbles.

4 Smear the whole of the cat's head with an even coat of petroleum jelly to stop the paper from sticking to the clay.

5 Tear some of the orange construction paper into small pieces and smear with paste, taking care not to make them too wet. Begin to cover the head with the paper, overlapping each piece.

6 When you have completely covered the head with orange paper, repeat the process with blue paper. Continue in this way, alternating the orange and blue, until you have applied seven layers. You should end with an orange layer.

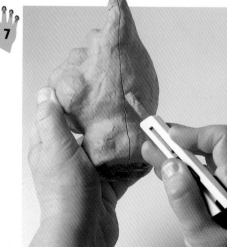

7 Leave to dry thoroughly. This may take some time, but you can speed things up by putting the head in a warm place. When it is dry, use a craft knife to cut cleanly all around the head. Make sure that the blade cuts through the paper and into the modeling clay beneath.

8 Prize the two halves of the head away from the modeling clay – they should come away quite easily.

9 Put some white glue on the rim of one of the halves.

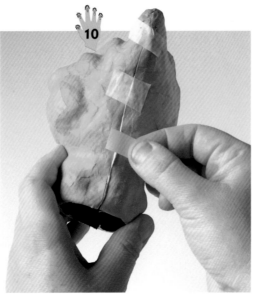

10 Carefully match the two halves together and hold them in place with small pieces of masking tape until the glue dries, which should take about 30 minutes.

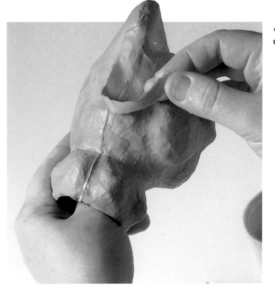

11 When the glue is dry, remove the masking tape and disguise the seam by pasting small pieces of torn orange paper over it so that they blend in with the rest of the head.

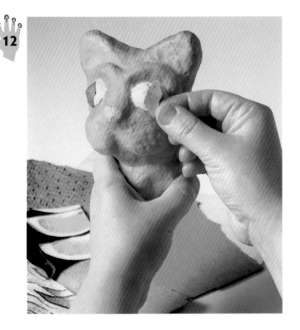

12 Tear some yellow paper, and paste it onto the eyeballs. Use some green paper to make the pupils of the eyes.

13 Glue some torn pieces of patterned orange paper onto the head. Cover the eyebrows and nose with blue paper and make a small mouth. Cover the collar with blue construction paper and the raised bobbles with alternate yellow and orange scraps of wrapping paper.

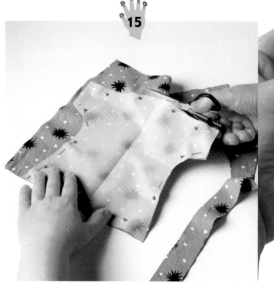

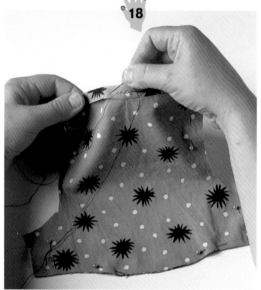

14 Trace the tunic template, cut it out, and pin it to a double thickness of fabric.

15 Carefully cut out the tunic.

16 Trace the hand templates, cut them out, and pin each of them to two pieces of felt. Cut them out.

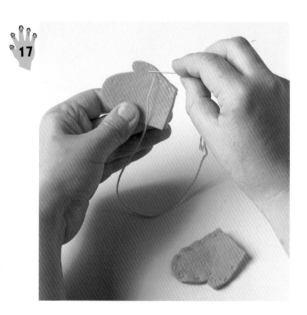

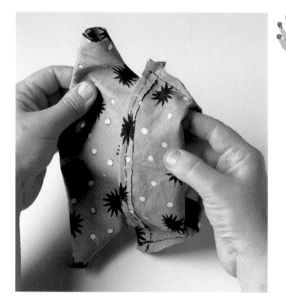

17 Make the hands by stitching the two layers of felt together with orange embroidery floss.

18 With the tunic still the wrong way out, turn up the hem and stitch the side, underarm, and shoulder seams together, leaving spaces at the neck and cuffs.

19 Turn the tunic right side out.

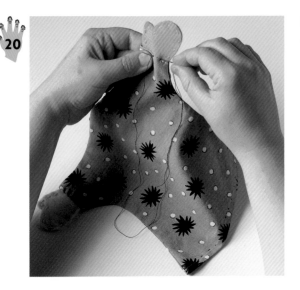

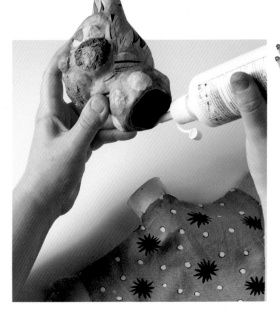

20 Turn the edge of the cuff to the inside, slot in the hand, and neatly stitch it in place. Repeat with the other hand.

21 Push a small section of cardboard tube into the neck of the tunic and glue it in place.

22 Apply some glue to the inside of the cat's head around the collar.

23 Push the head onto the cardboard tube, making sure that the collar covers the join with the tunic. Hold it in place until the glue is dry.

Crown Prince

• • •

This regal-looking character has rather humble origins — paper pulp and scrap material. Although it is a more elaborate puppet to make than some of the others, each stage is straightforward and requires no specialist technique or knowledge. The method is the one used to make traditional Punch-and-Judy-style puppets, and once you have mastered the approach you could easily make all the characters in a fairy story.

You will need
◊ Newspaper
◊ Cardboard tube
◊ Masking tape
◊ Papier-mâché pulp
◊ Knife
◊ Acrylic primer (white)
◊ Paintbrushes (small and medium)
◊ Acrylic paints (blue, pink, red, yellow, brown, and black)
◊ Plate or palette for mixing paints
◊ Gold paper or gold foil
◊ Scissors

◊ Clear, all-purpose glue
◊ Tracing paper
◊ Pencil
◊ Pins
◊ Gold-colored velvet, 2 pieces, 14 × 17 inches
◊ Needle
◊ Sewing thread
◊ 4 rubber bands
◊ Polyester stuffing
◊ White glue
◊ Gold-colored braid, 6 feet

Pants Template

Pants legs. Cut out four pants pieces using this template.

For the Prince's tunic, use the template for the Marmalade Cat, on page 26. Cut out 2 pieces of fabric.

1 Scrumple up a ball of newspaper so that it is the size of your fist. Secure the newspaper ball to the top of a cardboard tube with masking tape.

2 Evenly cover the newspaper with a layer of pulp. Use a purchased mix if you don't want to make your own. Smooth down the pulp onto the tube, which will form the neck, and leave to dry overnight.

3 Begin to model the nose, pressing the pulp well onto the head and smoothing out any seams. Add the eyes and eyebrows.

4 Make the lips and add a moustache and some hair. Model the crown simply by making even points around the head. When you have finished, leave the head to dry thoroughly, ideally for several days.

5 Use some more pulp to model the boots.

6 Make a clearly defined dent all around the top of each boot with a knife. The dent will make it easier to attach the pants legs later on. Leave to dry thoroughly.

7 Model the hands with pulp, remembering to make a separate thumb. Use a knife to make a dent around the wrists of both hands. Leave to dry.

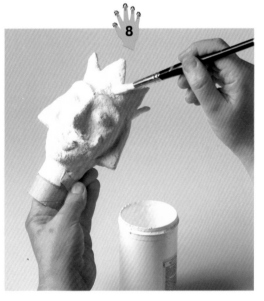

8 When the boots are dry, give them a coat of white acrylic primer. When the head is dry, give it a coat of white acrylic primer.

9 Use the medium paintbrush to paint the crown blue.

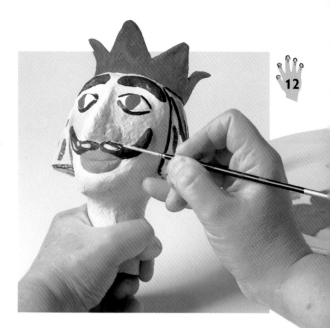

10 Paint the hair pale yellow and the face a skin tone. Make rosy cheeks by mixing red with the skin color on the face before it dries. Paint the lips bright red. Paint the eyes blue and the moustache and eyebrows dark brown. Add a dark brown line around the eyes.

11 Use a darker shade of yellow to add some rough streaks over the hair. When the paint is dry, add some dark brown lines.

12 Paint some fine, pale yellow lines on the moustache and eyebrows.

13 Paint the hands flesh pink.

14 Paint the boots blue, but paint the soles of the boots black.

15 Tear or cut out pieces of gold paper or foil and glue them to the points of the crown. Cut a long, narrow piece of foil to go around the base of the crown. Glue it in place.

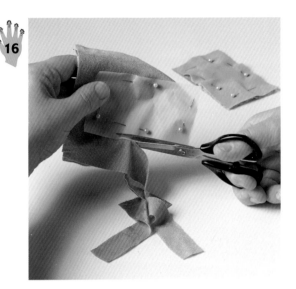

16 Trace and cut out the templates for the tunic and pants. Pin the templates onto two layers of the fabric, folded with right sides together.

17 Carefully cut out two legs and one tunic.

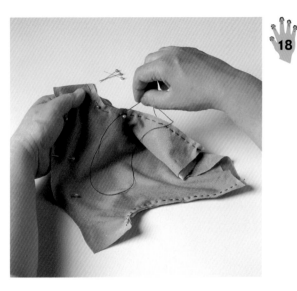

18 Use a neat running stitch to sew together the seams of the body and the pants legs.

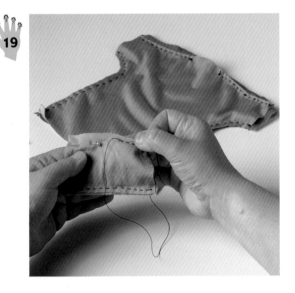

19 Remember not to sew up the cuffs or the top and bottom ends of the pants legs.

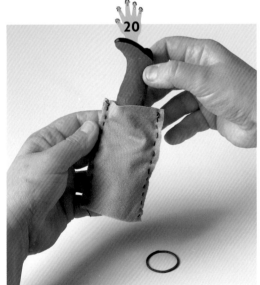

20 Push a boot into a pants leg so that the boot is completely covered by the pants leg.

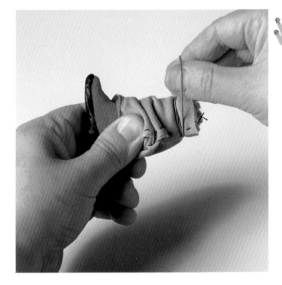

21 Wind a rubber band tightly around the boot where the dent is. Make sure the rubber band is as tight as possible.

22 Turn the pants leg right side out.

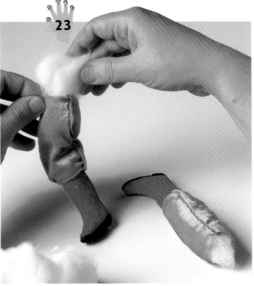

23 Put a little polyester stuffing in the leg, but do not fill it too full. Repeat for the other leg.

24 Push a hand, fingers first, into the cuff of the tunic, which is still inside out. Wind a rubber band tightly around the hand, making sure it rests in the ridge around the wrist. Make sure the rubber band is as tight as possible.

25 Repeat with the other hand, then turn the tunic right side out to reveal the firmly attached hands.

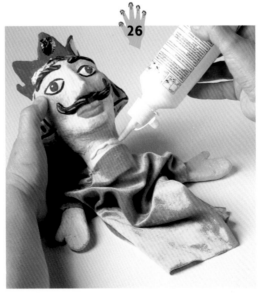

26 Smear some white glue around the neck and push the tunic onto the neck, over the line of glue.

27 Pin, then stitch the legs to the front of the bottom of the tunic.

28 Glue gold braid around the neck, cuffs, and down the front of the tunic.

29 Finally, glue braid around the hem of the tunic, covering the stitching that attaches the legs.

The Acrobat

· · ·

At last — here are simple instructions for making an articulated string puppet. These are usually quite complicated, technical projects; but when you make this acrobat, you make the joints at the same time you make the puppet, so all you need is patience. You can use a ready-made papier-mâché pulp if you do not want to make your own.

You will need
◊ Thin galvanized wire
◊ Wire cutters
◊ Pliers
◊ Newspaper
◊ Wallpaper paste
◊ Papier-mâché pulp
◊ Acrylic primer (white)
◊ Paintbrushes (medium and small)
◊ Acrylic paint (black, yellow, blue, and red)
◊ Clear all-purpose glue
◊ Stage hair

◊ Awl
◊ 2 lengths of wood, each ¾ × ¾ × 8 inches
◊ 1 length of wood, ¾ × ¾ × 12 inches
◊ Screw, approximately 1 inch long
◊ Screwdriver
◊ 7 eye hooks
◊ 2 lengths of strong thread, each approximately 20 inches
◊ 2 lengths of strong thread, each approximately 16 inches
◊ 1 length of strong thread, approximately 12 inches

1 Cut a length of wire approximately 2 feet long. Twist a loop in the middle of this — this will be the loop in the top of the puppet's head — and roughly wind the rest of the wire around itself to make a head shape. Leave a loop of wire at what will be the neck joint.

2 Thread a length of wire, a little longer than the first piece, through the loop at the bottom of the head and twist it to secure it; this will be the neck joint. Continue twisting and bending the wire to form the shape of the upper body. Make wire loops at the shoulders and waist.

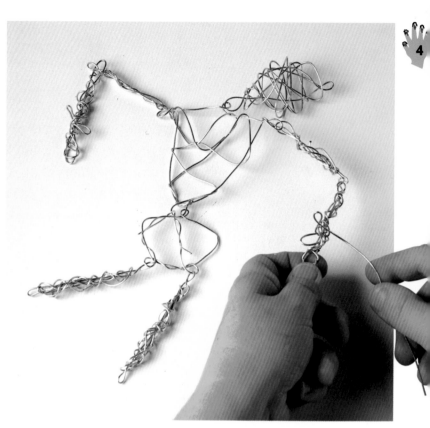

3 Use lengths of wire, each approximately 21 inches long, to make a pelvis, the upper arms, and the upper legs, attaching the limbs and body sections with loops of wire as before.

4 Add the lower arms and hands, using lengths of wire 25 inches long, leaving an upstanding loop of wire on each wrist, which are not jointed. These loops will be used to attach the arm strings.

5 Make the lower legs and feet in the same way, again using 25-inch lengths of wire. No loops are needed here because the leg strings are attached at the knees.

6 Tear a length of newspaper so that it is approximately 3 inches wide and smear it lightly on both sides with paste.

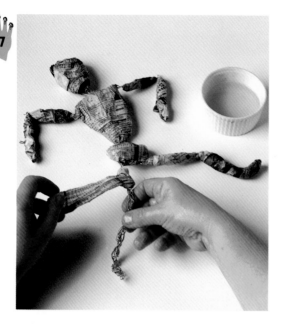

7 Start to wind the newspaper around all the sections of the puppet, making sure that you leave all the wire loop joints free. Use two layers to build up the shape of the body.

8 Begin to add paper pulp to the head and body, making sure that you add an even layer, about ¼ inch deep all over, although you can use more pulp to give the puppet more shape if necessary.

9 When you add pulp to the lower arm, take care that you keep the wire loop at the wrist free.

10 Use extra pulp to model the features on the face. Put the puppet in a warm place – an oven on a very low setting, for example – and leave to dry thoroughly.

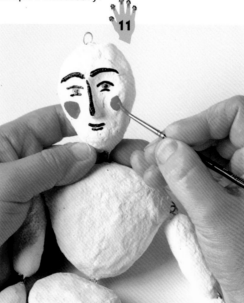

11 When it is dry, paint the whole puppet with one coat of acrylic primer. Use the small paintbrush to paint blue eyes, black pupils and eyebrows, and the nose and mouth. Paint on red spots for the cheeks.

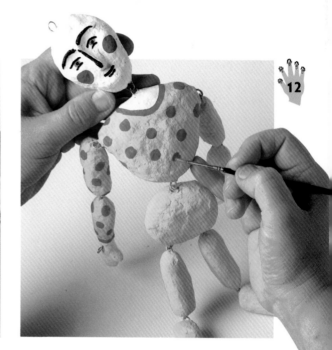

12 Paint the puppet's upper legs, the arms as far as the wrists, and the body as far as the neck yellow. Paint a red outline around the neck, wrists, and lower legs, then paint red dots on the yellow costume.

13 Carefully paint black ballet shoes on the puppet's feet.

14 Smear some glue over the top of the head. Arrange some stage hair on the glue on the head and hold it in place until the glue is dry. Make sure the loop of wire at the top of the head is not covered with hair.

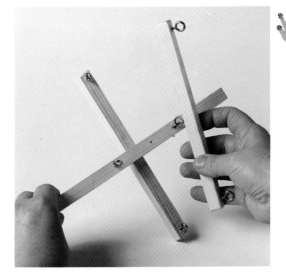

15 Use an awl to make a hole in the center of the longer piece of wood and in the center of one of the shorter pieces of wood.

16 Screw these two lengths of wood firmly together.

17 Using eye hooks to form a moving joint, attach the other length of wood. Attach the remaining eye hooks.

18 Attach lengths of strong thread to the loops at the knees (approximately 20 inches), at the wrists (approximately 16 inches) and at the top of the head (approximately 12 inches). Fasten the knots tightly.

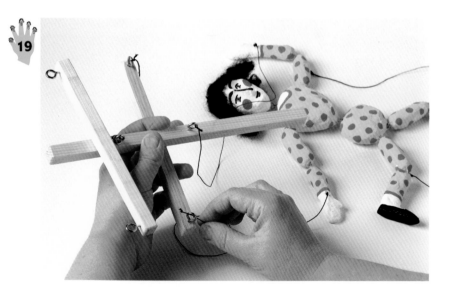

19 Attach the other ends of the strings to the loops on the lengths of wood. The leg strings are joined to the moving section of wood; the arm strings are attached to the fixed section; and the head string is attached to the eye hook set just behind the crosspiece that holds the arm strings.

Supermarket Shocker

Be more creative with your trash. You can make some extraordinary characters from the mass of throwaway packaging that finds its way into our trash cans every day. You might even find yourself looking along the supermarket shelves for interesting shapes that you can transform into extraterrestrial puppets.

You will need
◊ Large plastic bottle (we used a ½-gallon bottle)
◊ Craft knife
◊ Paper or fabric dishcloth
◊ Thin piece of wood with rounded end (we used a chopstick)
◊ Plastic squeezy lemon
◊ Scissors
◊ 2 bottle tops
◊ Small block of wood
◊ Hole punch
◊ 2 paper brads

1 Using a craft knife, carefully cut away the back section (that is, opposite to the handle) of the plastic bottle.

2 Again using the craft knife, make a series of small slits around the top of what will be the head of your puppet.

3 Cut the paper dishcloth into strips, approximately ½ inch wide.

4 Fold a cut strip in two and push it into the slit with the rounded end of a thin piece of wood.

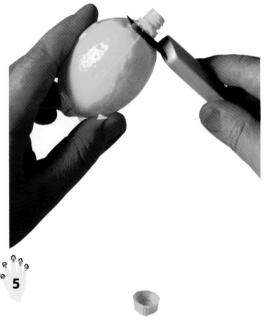

5 Cut off the screw-top from the plastic lemon.

6 Cut the lemon in half lengthwise; there is usually a line to follow.

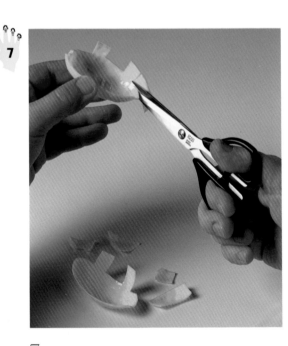

7 Cut each half of the lemon into ear shapes, leaving small tabs to attach them to the head. Remember to cut each shape differently to fit the right and left sides.

8 Cut slots in the sides of the bottle head to correspond with the ears, bearing in mind that the handle of the bottle will be the nose.

9 Push the ear tabs into the slots in the head.

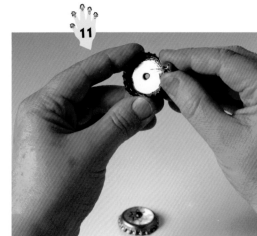

10 Place a bottle top on the block of wood and pierce a hole through the center with the hole punch.

11 Push a paper brad through the hole in the bottle top.

12 Use the hole punch to make holes in the front of the face, one on each side of the handle.

13 Place a bottle-top eye over the hole and hold it in place by pushing the tabs of the paper brad through the hole and, with your hand inside the bottle, pressing open the tabs. Repeat with the other eye.

Felt Friends

These small finger puppets are an ideal way to use up scraps of felt that you might have left over from some of the other projects. Make them as bright and jolly as you can. You could add sequins, beads, jewels or feathers to make them look more elaborate.

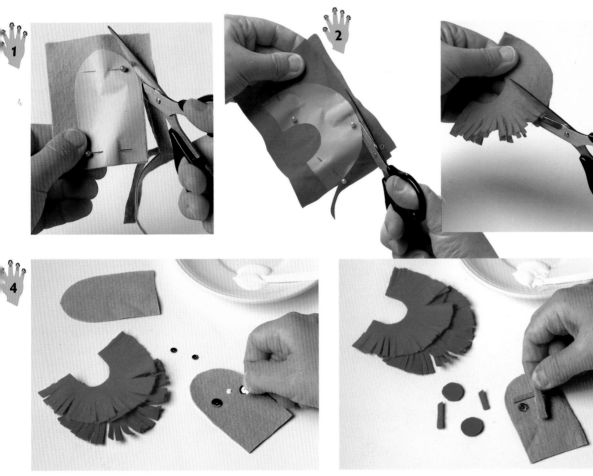

Cut out two pieces of felt using this template.

Felt Friends Templates

Cut out two pieces of felt using this template.

1 Trace and cut out the templates. Pin the body template to the green felt. Cut out two pieces.

2 Cut out one pink hair shape and one red hair shape.

3 Cut the longer sides of the red and pink felt shapes into bangs.

4 Glue sequins to the front of one of the green felt body pieces to make eyes, using a large sequin underneath and a smaller one on top for the pupil.

5 Cut small strips of orange felt and glue them to the face as eyebrows and a nose.

You will need
◊ Tracing paper
◊ Pencil
◊ Pins
◊ Felt (green, pink, red, orange)
◊ Sequins
◊ Fabric glue

6 Glue the red cheeks in place.

7 Position the pink hair on the inside of the back body piece. Glue it down.

8 Glue the red hair directly on top of the pink hair.

9 Glue the green body piece with the face on it to the back body piece so that the red and pink hair pieces are sandwiched between, with just the bangs showing.

Finger Family

What could be simpler than to convert an old glove into a family of whimsical characters? Each one has its own expression and entertaining hairstyle. You might want to have a happy family on one hand and a miserable family on the other.

You will need
◊ 1 wool glove (we used an orange glove)
◊ White sequins
◊ Small black beads
◊ Needle
◊ Sewing thread
◊ 1 piece of ¾-inch wooden dowel, approximately 12 inches long
◊ Darning needle
◊ Tapestry yarn (black, yellow, orange, green, pink, and blue)
◊ Scissors

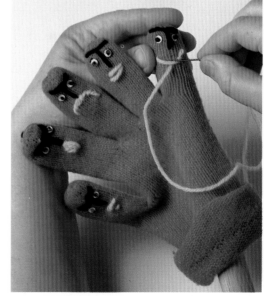

1 Put the glove on and sew white sequins and black beads onto each finger as eyes.

2 Push the piece of dowel into each finger in turn to support it while you sew.

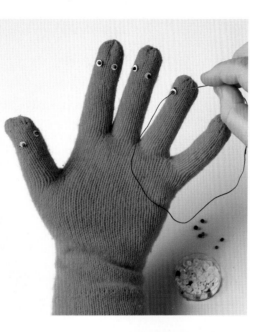

3 Use black tapestry yarn to sew eyebrows and the line of a nose on each face. Stitch the nose straight down between the sequin eyes.

4 Sew on the mouth with yellow yarn, changing the expression on each finger.

5 Using a different color for each finger, sew loops of tapestry yarn to make the hair.

6 Trim the loops of hair evenly around each face.